# WHAT'S MY DOG SAYING?

Keeping Children and Dogs Safe.

## NICKOLA ENGEL

Illustrated by Susan Shorter

"Sam, Sam, help me," screamed Josh as he jumped off the swings and onto the climbing frame.

"What's wrong?" asked Sam, concerned about his friend.

"It's the dog; it's trying to get me," he said whilst trying to catch his breath.

Sam saw a dog running up to them, but he watched it run past to catch its ball and then run back to its owner.

"It's okay, Josh. The dog wasn't chasing you; it was just running to catch its ball."

"Phew," Josh replied, "I was really scared."

Josh was a new child in Sam's class, and they had soon become friends. They loved playing together, but they always had to play at the park or at Josh's house because Sam and his mummy had two dogs. Josh was very scared of them. He didn't like dogs at all.

"You know what, Josh? I think we need to stop you from being scared of dogs so you can have fun in the park and not worry about them. And then you can sleepover at my house," said Sam with a smile.

"I'm not sure if I'm brave enough, Sam. They really scare me."

"Okay, well, how about we just try? I can teach you lots about dogs so you might not be so scared."

"Um, okay," said Josh. "We can try."

Sam had loved dogs since he was a baby, and his mummy worked as a dog trainer. She had taught him so much about them. He loved his two dogs, Louie and Scruffy, and they were the best of friends.

The boys headed to Josh's house for some milk and cookies, and Sam said Joshua was ready for his first lesson.

Sam explained to Josh that dogs have some of the same feelings that people do.

"They can get cross, worried, and excited, Josh, just like we can. But they have different ways of showing us."

"You see, Sam, that's the problem. They can't tell me what they are feeling. They just seem not to like me, and they bark at me," said Josh.

"But they can tell you what they are feeling, and they do all the time," Sam continued. "You just need to know what to look for."

"I'm not sure I understand," Josh replied.

Sam explained that for Josh to know how a dog was feeling, he needed to look at the way it was holding its body. He explained that Josh needed to look at its face, legs, body, and tail.

"The different body parts will show you little clues. When you put them together, they will give you the full picture."

"Oh, I see," said Josh. "That's clever. So, what should I look for then?"

"Well, I guess we can start with the head and face. That's where a dog will mostly tell you how it feels. And since that's the part where the teeth are, that's the part you need to pay extra attention to," replied Sam. "When a dog is happy, its ears, mouth, and eyes relax, and it has a happy look."

Sam continued to explain that when a dog is scared, it pins its ears back flat against its head, and its eyes become big and wide. It may also pant. "Sometimes," Sam added, "if a dog is really scared, it may growl as a warning for what is scaring it to keep away. A dog's whole body will tense, and it may look like it is leaning on its back legs."

"Now," said Sam, "this can be the scary bit, but don't worry. I will tell you what you can do so that you may never have to see a dog act that way."

"Oh, I'm not sure I want to know," Josh replied.

"But this is the most important part," said Sam. "You need to know this to be safe around dogs."

"Okay," said Josh in a worried tone.

"There are times when a dog can be aggressive," continued Sam, "even when it isn't scared. It might just be that someone has gotten into its space, and it doesn't want that person there. You can spot this, as the dog will fix its eyes and stare, point its ears up and forward, put more of its weight forward onto its front feet, and most likely growl. It may even curl its lips to show front teeth.

"Can we stop now, Sam? I'm so scared."

"But that's the worse bit over now, Josh."

"But what should I do if I see a dog doing all those things?" Josh asked whilst burying his head in his arms.

"Well," replied Sam, "the hardest part will be fighting your desire to run away. If a dog is being aggressive and you run, it may chase after you. It may seem a bit scary, but all you need to do is stand still. Don't look into its eyes. Keep your body as relaxed as you can. This will show the dog that you don't mean it any harm. It should start to calm down, and then all you need to do is back away slowly and calmly. If the dog is scared, stop what you are doing and walk away from it."

"But why do dogs have to do all that, Sam? I don't understand."

"Okay," Sam replied, "do you remember when Kiera came round with her mummy the other day when we were playing, and all she wanted to do was jump all over me?"

"Yes, I remember."

"Well, I asked her to stop nicely, didn't I? But she didn't, so I got cross and shouted at her to leave us alone."

"That's right," Josh agreed.

"So, you see Josh, that's what dogs do too. They can't shout at us to leave them alone like we shout, so they use their bodies instead."

"Oh, I see, Sam. I thought they were just being mean and naughty."

"No," said Sam, "not at all. It's just how they communicate to us and each other."

"Now that you put it like that," Josh said with a smile on his face, "I think I understand."

"What else should I look for?" asked Josh.

Sam told Josh that another important part of a dog's body is its tail. He said that when a dog is happy, it holds its tail in a relaxed position and wags it swiftly from side to side.

He then explained that when a dog is scared, it holds its tail flat against its bottom or even between its legs.

"So, what about when a dog is being grumpy?" asked Josh as he gave a little giggle at calling them grumpy.

"When a dog is really grumpy," replied Sam, "it holds its tail very stiff and as high as possible."

"Oh right," said Josh. "I didn't realise dogs were so clever."

"They really are," replied Sam. "Dogs don't like to fight or bite other dogs or humans and will only do it if they have no other options. Before that, though, they use body language to stop confrontations. They really do make wonderful pets, Josh. They just need to be treated with kindness and respect."

"So, how do you properly treat a dog with respect?" asked Josh curiously.

"Ah, now that's the easy part," answered Sam. "Never hit or shout at a dog. Never approach one that is sleeping, and don't get into a dog's bed. That's its bed, and it may not want to share. Leave a dog alone while it is eating, and don't take toys or bones from it."

"That does sound easy," agreed Josh.

"See, I told you. If you do all of those things, a dog won't really need to be grumpy with you."

It was time to go home, so Sam and Josh said goodbye. But to Sam's surprise, Josh asked to meet his dogs.

"Of course you can," said Sam with a big grin on his face. "I'll bring Louie. He is very soft and gentle."

The next day Sam and Josh met at the park. Sam had Louie on lead while Josh walked cautiously over to them. Josh stood so that the see-saw was between himself and Sam with Louie.

"I'm too scared to come over," called Josh.

"That's okay," replied Sam. "Just try to remember what I taught you yesterday."

Josh went over yesterday's lesson in his head. "Shall I look at his body language?" he asked.

"Yes," answered Sam.

Josh calmed his nerves and looked at Louie's face, body, and tail. Louie's face looked relaxed, his body was relaxed with his weight even on all four paws, and his tail was relaxed but wagging. "I think that he is happy," Josh called to Sam. "Is that right?"

"That is right," Sam replied. "Well done."

Josh was becoming less nervous now and decided to take a few steps closer.

"You're doing it, Josh," Sam said encouragingly. "Now, when you get really close, just bend down ever so slightly and offer the back of your hand for him to sniff. That's how dogs like to be greeted by strangers."

"Okay," replied Josh. He took a deep breath and did as instructed.

Josh laughed. "That tickles."

Once Louie had sniffed Josh's hand, Sam told him it was now okay to give Louie a scratch under the chin. Louie liked the fuss and had thanked Josh by licking his hand.

"This is awesome," said Josh. "I never thought I would get this close to a dog."

Josh was so pleased with what had happened that when he got home, he told his mum all about it, and she was very proud of him.

"Tomorrow," Josh added excitedly, "I'm going to meet Sam's other dog, Scruffy."

"That's great news. I'm so proud of you," his mum replied. "Sam is such a good friend."

Josh ran round to Sam's house the next morning and knocked on the door. Sam came out to meet him.

"I'm ready," Josh declared.

"Brilliant," replied Sam. "One thing, though. Scruffy loves people, but he can get a little overexcited when he meets someone new."

"What do you mean by overexcited?" Josh asked, feeling a little nervous again.

"Well, he might jump up at you," answered Sam.

"Oh dear, I'm not sure I'm ready for that," replied Josh.

Sam explained to Josh that he wouldn't let Scruffy hurt him and that he was perfectly safe.

Sam went on to say, "When a dog jumps up at you and you don't like it because you aren't sure if it is friendly or not, turn your back on it and stand still. It's called being a tree. You will seem very boring to the dog, and it will stop."

Sam also said that when Josh is very scared, he should crouch down on the floor and tuck his head under his arms. "It's called being a stone. Again, this will bore a dog, and it will leave you alone."

"Okay, I understand now," Josh said. "I think I can do this."

"Excellent," replied Sam. "But remember that we can come back outside if you need to."

The boys went into Sam's house. Louie was in the kitchen, and Scruffy was in the garden, playing with his ball. Louie came up to them and wagged his tail, so Josh said hello and gave him a scratch under the chin.

"I think he remembers me," commented Josh with a giggle.

"Yes, he does," Sam replied. "So, are you ready to meet Scruffy now?" he asked.

Taking a deep breath in, Josh nodded his head.

Sam opened the door, and scruffy ran in and headed straight for Josh.

Josh was very scared, but he remembered what Sam had said to him. He shouldn't run away, and he should just turn around with his back towards the dog. So, as soon as Scruffy jumped up, Josh did as instructed.

But Scruffy was a clever dog. He ran round to the front of Josh again and jumped up. Josh simply turned around again.

It took a couple of tries, but Scruffy soon thought that this was very boring. So, he stopped and walked away and then gave a big shake.

"I did it; I did it!" said Josh with a massive smile on his face.

"You were totally amazing, Josh, and very brave," commented Sam.

Once Josh had calmed down a bit from his excitement, he remembered that when Scruffy had walked away, he gave a big shake.

"Why did he do that, Sam?" he asked. "I thought dogs only did that when they were wet."

Sam explained to Josh that it was a calming signal.

"What's a calming signal?"

"Calming signals are certain movements or actions that a dog will use when it is stressed, overexcited, or when another dog or person is stressed or overexcited."

"Oh, I see," said Josh. "So, because Scruffy was still overexcited when he stopped jumping up, he shook to calm himself down?"

"That's exactly right," Sam replied.

paw lift

lip licking

scratching

"Wow," Josh said, "that really is so clever. What do these calming signals look like?"
"There are actually quite a lot," answered Sam, "but the easiest ones are these."

yawning

sniff the ground

look away

Josh was so amazed. He never knew that dogs had so many ways to communicate.

"I can't tell you how much better I feel about dogs now," said Josh as he gave his friend a big hug.

"Thank you so much."

"You're very welcome," Sam replied smiling.

That weekend the boys went to the park again to play.
Before long they saw the dog that had been chasing its ball and had scared Josh.
"There's that dog again, Sam, but I'm not scared anymore," Josh said with a giggle.
"Awesome," said Sam.

**So, kids, just remember the following:**

| Never | Always |
|---|---|
| • shout at or hit a dog; | • be gentle; |
| • take its food or toys; | • leave a dog to eat alone; |
| • get into its bed; | • give it space; |
| • disturb a sleeping dog; | • let it sleep; |
| • run away when scared; or | • walk away calmly, or be a tree or stone; and |
| • ignore what a dog is trying to tell you. | • watch for signs of stress and calming signals. |

# The End

Printed in Great Britain
by Amazon